The Family Memory Project

The present of the past… for the future

Dr Rie Natalenko

The Family Memory Project

Copyright © 2014 Dr Rie Natalenko

All rights reserved. No part of this book may be reproduced or transmitted in any form or by any means without written permission from the author.

ISBN 978-0-9941732-1-8

Dedication

This book is for my parents, Charles and Alice Widdowson. I value their stories and have learned so much from them. They taught me that family comes first, and should always be there for you, no matter what. I hope I have passed that on to my own children.

It is also for my husband, Bob. He has supported me in all the crazy things I have wanted to do with my life, including writing this book and working to get it out into the world.

It is for my children. Just about everything parents do is for their children, but this may help them to appreciate the value of their parents' and grandparents' stories.

It is for those people who have aging parents and who want to start gathering their stories. This book will make it easier for you.

Additional thanks are due to Xenia Lo for her excellent advice and ideas, to Judeth Wilson for her unfailing support and encouragement, and to Brendon Burchard whose teaching made this all possible.

Table of Contents

The Family Memory Project 1

Dedication 3

Foreword 7

Introduction 9

Chapter 1: Why is this so important? 15

Chapter 2: What do I say when they make excuses? 29

Chapter 3: So what steps I should take? 39

Chapter 4: Preparation – let's get started! 43

Chapter 5: The process – let's record the memories! 51

Chapter 6 Putting it together – let's organise the memories! 63

Chapter 7 Publishing Audio Memories 79

Chapter 8 Publishing Written Memories 85

Chapter 9 Publishing Video Memories 95

Chapter 10: Other Ideas for Publishing 99

Conclusion: So what do I do right now? 103

References and Resources 109

Testimonials 111

Foreword

We always knew our daughter was special and, in the writing of this book, she has proved this to be true. A project such as this takes time, effort and lots of love.

After reading *The Family Memory Project* we were amazed, for not only is it interesting to read, it is informative, helpful, so very clearly presented and an attainable CHALLENGE for anyone desiring to leave a legacy for their families.

When Rie came for a few days to record our voices and we made comments as we watched our DVD, we were both surprised at the events we could remember concerning incidents which took place so long ago. It was a joy, and an exhilarating experience or, as Rie would possibly say, 'An *adventure* into past memories.'[1]

When you read this book, we pray that you, and many more, will take up the exciting challenge to jog those memories! It's fun and it's fruitful just jogging memories from the computer of our lives, lived to the full, so that future generations might be blessed.

Well done, Rie, we are proud of you.

Charles and Alice Widdowson

---

[1] One day, when Dad was driving me to the airport to catch a plane home, we became lost. Dad was a little flustered, so, in an attempt to reframe the experience, I said, "Try to think of it as an adventure." They have never let me forget that!

Introduction

Have you ever lost someone close? Maybe a parent or grandparent?

It's devastating. You miss them. There's an emptiness inside where they once were…

…and so much is lost.

All their life is gone forever. Everything they learned, everything they could have shared with you and your children is gone.

As your loved ones age, their memories fade, and when they die, those memories will be lost forever.

That's why I decided to write this book, and put together the Family Memory Kit. I wanted to help people to preserve the memories that are their legacy.

This is your heritage and the heritage of your children.

If you can help your relatives to gather and preserve their memories, then it can give you and your children a better understanding of who you are and where you came from. It may hold lessons that can inspire your family into the future. It's worth preserving, don't you think?

"Chaque vieillard qui meurt, c'est une bibliothèque qui brûle." ("Every old man that dies, is a library that burns.") M. Amadou Hampate-Ba

In the past, societies valued their elders. They were the keepers of tradition. Theirs were the words of wisdom that the young people listened to. Theirs were the stories that kept the society strong.

Today, in Western society, we are isolated. Because of family mobility and the need for jobs, we move away from our families. Very seldom do we have that extended family to turn to. Older people are more and more isolated and alone, they neither have support nor can be the support for their grandchildren and great grandchildren.

Yet there is a deep sense of emptiness within us. As we get older, we feel that something is missing. That is why ancestry.com is so popular, why people are researching their family trees, why programs such as Who Do You Think You Are? and Find my Family are watched so avidly. We long for that connection to the past which our lifestyle has ripped away from us.

How important is it, then, to preserve the lives, the memories, the stories of our parents, before they are lost forever?

It is easier, with modern technology, than it ever was before.

For the first time in history, you can record a person's life stories with simple, inexpensive recording equipment. Most phones have a recorder built in. Most computers will record a voice. Digital recorders are easy to find and very inexpensive. With this technology, you can easily make records of your parents' and grandparents' memories.

Once the recordings are made, you can publish them for the family in many, many ways. The traditional way would be to write them down, but these days you can have them transcribed, keep them as audio recordings on CDs, put them onto websites, add pictures as slide shows, make digital stories, use them in scrapbooks and photobooks - the possibilities are endless. This book will explain how to do all of these and more.

This is your family legacy.

The process of recording memories gives you a reason to get closer to your family – both in the gathering of the information and in the sharing. It can build bridges, provide answers, be fun and lead to understanding, closeness and healing.

I always promised myself that I would sit down with my Nana and write her stories. Sadly, work and motherhood took up all my time and I never did. For many years I regretted that. Then, recently, I realised that I was in the same position with my parents. I knew some of their stories, but not enough. They had written some of those stories down, but not many of them. They had told many more stories of their lives over the years, and there was no record of those stories.

So I made a decision to begin. I edited their old super 8 films onto a DVD. Then I went to Melbourne, where they live, and we sat down together and I helped them to record the voice-over for those films. It was a joyful and very moving experience, and it led me to realise that there was, or should be, a sense of urgency for everyone around me to do the same, and more, before all our family memories are lost.

There is no reason why you, too, can't start the process of collecting memories. You don't have to imagine it as a huge life story. I am not suggesting that you write the biography of your mother or father - although you certainly can do that, if you feel you would like to. What I am suggesting is rather a "collection of recollections," a gathering of memories.

For some of us, that may be the best we can hope for. If parents are fading, and their memories becoming confused and jumbled, maybe capturing a few of them is the most we can expect – but it is better than nothing – and it emphasises the need for action NOW.

Who knows how long we have? Nana was always so strong and she seemed immortal to me when I was young and naive. She faded so fast, and I had a sick newborn, and she lived 10 hours drive away. The opportunity was lost.

For years as a writer in the community, and as a film-school teacher, I have helped people to tell their stories. So instead of wasting all that experience and knowledge, I have gathered it here so everyone can share it, and act in their own lives to preserve their parents' memories.

In this book, and in the Family Memory Kit, I have put together a step-by-step process to make it a simple and infinitely rewarding task to capture and preserve memories.

This book will cover:

- The reasons for gathering the stories, and how to overcome the objections you might experience.
- What to do in order to prepare for the process.
- The step-by-step process - with checklists and lists of questions, triggers and prompts.
- The possibilities for getting those stories out there.
- If you want to write it up, the steps needed to write a series of memoirs or even a full-length biography.
- If you want to put it together in a different form, using a different medium, the step-by-step process for each different way.
- If you prefer to have it done by someone else, you'll be pointed in the right direction.

But it is important to start now. Don't put this off as I did with my Nana, until it was too late. If we all start now, we can make ourselves the custodians of our family history. We can take upon ourselves the joyful task of preserving our children's heritage, so we can share with our children, our grandchildren, our nieces and nephews, those stories and memories and traditions that are their heritage and legacy.

We can give them the present of the past, for the future.

Chapter 1: Why is this so important?

When we are children, we think that the way we live is the way everybody lives. We don't know what goes on behind the doors down our street, never mind what goes on across town, across the country or in other places in the world. Neither do we know what went on behind the same doors 20 years ago, 30, 40 50, or 100 years ago. We don't know the ways our parents coped with the joys and disappointments and trials and tragedies in their lives, how they lived, how they loved, how they suffered.

Yet that part is our heritage. It is part of where we come from. It is part of who we are.

As we begin to hear those stories, we have fresh insights into how our family shaped us. We begin to understand who we are and why we are like that. We begin to understand the closeness and rifts in families, why certain members were drawn together and others pulled or pushed apart.

I have two warnings about this journey, before we go any further.

1. The emotional journey

It can be a huge emotional journey, collecting a parent's memories and piecing them together, but it will mean a great deal to your family.

When I say "family", I don't mean just a nuclear family of parents and children. Nor am I referring only to an extended family with grandparents, uncles, aunts, nieces and nephews – although I do mean that sort of family, too. Today there are so many types of family, all equally important. Close friends, alternative families, gay and lesbian families, mixed race families – and they all share love and a multitude of cultures and ideas in their heritage.

For some people, the journey may be harder than for others. Some people may be orphans or may have grown up in an atypical family, or felt that they were somehow alienated from their families. For those people and others, it might be that this process of collecting memories from ageing family members is painful.

Every family is unique. Each family has its own strengths and weaknesses. In every family, though, collecting these stories can be a path to healing and understanding. At first, there may be difficulty finding compassion for some family members, but while the process may not entirely change anyone's point of view, it often helps people to see their families from different angles.

You may also discover stories that you didn't know, and uncover feelings that you didn't expect. Each story adds a lens through which you can see yourself, and through which other family members can see themselves.

2. The responsibility

This is the first time that we have been able to record someone's memories so easily and so fully, in their own voice. This means we have a huge responsibility for the future. We have to take on the responsibility for the preservation of that history.

We must digitise as much as possible, so that it doesn't deteriorate any more than it already has, and before the technology changes so much that it becomes impossible to retrieve the information. It is vital to do this before the photos fade or are torn or damaged, before the videos deteriorate beyond recovery, before cassette tapes break or stretch or the tape sticks together. All must be digitised (put onto computer) and preserved as soon as possible to prevent their deterioration or accidental destruction.

I stored some photos on floppy disk that I will probably never be able to recover – if I haven't accidentally thrown away the disk! My wedding photos were on slides which we kept in the attic. Some of them are ruined, and most are faded and blue.

Don't allow either the fears of the emotional journey or the magnitude of the responsibility stop you, though. The ease with which we can collect these memories today makes the task even more exciting.

It's exciting because you'll discover so many important and interesting things about your past and your parents' place in the family, the community and in history.

Everyone's a significant person in the world. It's actually the little things that make people so special. To know what your grandmother was wearing the day she met your grandfather, how he proposed, and what the family thought of him – these details bring your own story to life.

The relative that you're interviewing may not think that you'll find that sort of thing interesting, but you know that you will. The story is a snapshot of history. It's fascinating to find out how customs have changed, how the attitudes of the past are different from those of today. However, there are other reasons besides curiosity to ask questions and record the answers. Preserving their stories recognises the worthiness of your relatives, your love and respect for them. They are sharing the lessons they have learned, sharing the wisdom they have gained, and it is your inheritance.

You'll get an insight into their humanity. The times were different, but you'll discover that in many ways they were the same. Your parents defied their parents, too. They had their own hopes and desires, their own triumphs, and there may be things they did about which they may still feel ashamed. They may not tell you about those. However, whatever they share, you'll understand them better and you'll become closer.

It will help them, too. Sharing their past has helped many people to put their life in order, to connect to their past self, to relive happy times, to discover what matters and to set the record straight.

It's a sad fact that most people won't get around to doing this. They'll miss out on this wonderful opportunity that you are contemplating. What a loss! I'm sure that you've heard people say, "I've spent so many years learning to do (whatever) and when I die, it will all be lost." Maybe you've even said that yourself. There are so many wonderful things that we learn in our lives – skills, knowledge, wisdom. They'll all be lost if we don't make a distinct effort to record them.

I have sometimes looked at a photo with me in it, and I have no recollection of where or when it was taken. I can't even remember the names of the people who were in it with me. We put so many memories into the dark recesses of our mind, never to be thought of again. Imagine having a way to jog those memories back into the present. That is what this project will help you to do.

I once found a box of old photos in a garage sale – pictures of babies, of a family that I didn't know growing up somewhere that looked like Europe. I asked the stallholder whose they were, and she answered,

"Just some old photos I found when I helped to clear a house after the old lady had died."

Those photos represented lost memories. I felt very sad looking at them. I imagined the old lady looking back at those photos of her children, her grandchildren growing up. Was that her, perhaps, laughing on the beach? Nobody would ever look at them again and relive those times.

If you don't help your relatives to pass on their memories, will you regret it one day? What will you answer when your own children ask about their heritage?

No matter what the topic, or how trivial the stories may seem, one day someone in your family will read them or watch them or listen to them and understand more of their own heritage. Preserving family memories is a gift to them. It is a gift only you can give.

That's why it's so important to encourage your ageing relatives to share their stories with you.

There's one more idea that I'd like you to consider, which is that while a person's memories may only be of interest at first to their own family, in time they could be important historical documents. It may be important in the greater scheme of things to discover what ordinary people thought of the period of history in which they lived, and of the events they experienced. It could become a resource which is important to the whole world in the future.

You can learn from what you discover, share what your relatives share with you, be blessed by the insights and the joys that you record.

People are desperate today to learn where they came from, and family memories can help them to understand the past. Family memories can help to recognise why choices were made that helped to shape the direction that the family took, helped them to become what they are today, where they fit in the larger picture of family history.

It's important to encourage your relatives to remember where and how they lived, what they learned and why they believe what they do. You are part of the "middle" generation, bridging the distance between the past and the future, strengthening the bonds between the generations.

If you've gone through the pain of loss already, you can appreciate the importance of preserving what you can, so that you can save what needs to be saved.

You may have already made that decision – to help one of your ageing relatives tell their story. If you have, you will discover that as you are a character in their stories, so they become more fully rounded characters in your own. You will gain deeper insights into the way you relate to them than you ever thought could be possible.

If you're ready to take that journey, then this book (and the Family Memory Kit) will be there to help you step by step along the way.

Nearly 24 years ago, I sat with a group of year 11 students who were embarking on a new venture. They would spend one day a week helping out in a retirement home, a preschool or working with developmentally disabled adults. They would spend a term at each placement. When we discussed the retirement home, the questions were many:

- What do we talk about?
- Do they really want us there?
- How can we relate to old people?

It turned out that less than half of the group had grandparents that they saw regularly. They were wary of what they might encounter – I don't think they imagined that they'd form any bond with the residents. Amazingly, that was what happened. They loved hearing the stories that the elderly residents would tell. One girl, Maria, was delighted to report that the lady she'd taken for a walk had told her about the time that she stole some stockings from a shop to wear at a dance. She whispered to Maria about the American soldiers coming to Sydney and how lots of Australian girls had shown them how patriotic they were!

Each day after placement, the students would say how it went, and what they did or learned. Some of the stories the students heard were heartbreaking – how one man had outlived his wife and four children, and his grandchildren never came to visit. Some were inspiring – one of the residents had been a swimmer in the Commonwealth Games. Some were deliciously subversive, like the lady who "showed the Americans her patriotism!"

At the end of the year, many of the students reported that this was their favourite placement, because they grew close to the elderly residents and were really interested in the stories they had to tell.

One day I was telling my daughter's teacher at the primary school about the program, and he had a great idea. He set up a "surrogate grandchildren" project for their year 5 and 6 students, where the children visited the nursing home once a week, and spent time talking to the residents. It was a huge success. It was hard to tell who benefitted most – the students who rarely saw their grandparents, or the residents who enjoyed the company of the children.

The whole idea moved me to become a community historian, collecting oral histories and writing them down. Then in 2006 I attended a "train the trainer" course at the Australian Centre for the Moving Image, where I learned how to record digital stories. That motivated me to teach people how to add images to the stories that they told. I was hooked!

I worked on many projects – the Memory and Place Lake Illawarra project, where I was honoured to help a 'young man' in his nineties, Sonny Massey, record his stories. I worked on a project which recorded the memories of growing up in the Barnardos homes after the war. I worked with people who had come through depression, with survivors of brain cancer, with Vietnam Vets and ageing gay men. With each project, I felt honoured to share the stories and to help record them.

I must admit that at first, everything was a bit trial-and-error. However, as time went on, it became clear that some things worked better than others, some techniques were more successful, some questions more fruitful. I realised that the process could be simple, enjoyable, and was in no way a chore. It was a privilege to hear the stories and it was amazing how much I learned as I listened and recorded.

I worked out a system, and a series of questions and prompts and memory triggers which worked really well. It's amazing, as people travel back with you to moments in the past, how much they remember – and how much they will share!

I helped my mother-in-law to record her memories. She recorded them in Russian. After she died, my husband translated them and he and my sister-in-law wrote the book Lilya's Journey which was published by Simon & Shuster in 2004.

I'm often asked to speak about memoir writing to various groups – mostly to residents of aged care homes or to church groups for the more senior members of their congregations. It's great to get them enthusiastic about recording their stories. However, as I speak to people of my own generation – people whose relatives are getting on in years – I know in my heart that I've found my real audience. It's sometimes hard for the elderly to tackle the memoir "thing" on their own. It takes a while to convince them that there's any point, and they come up with a myriad of excuses – which I will address in the next chapter in case you come up against similar arguments. I know I don't have much of a job to convince you that this is an important undertaking.

In this world where time is flying past so fast, if we don't act soon it will be too late. This is the time to act. This is a book – a method – which will help you to help them. I'm convinced that for many people this is the ideal way to do it. If you wait until your ageing relatives "get around to" writing their memoirs, you'll be waiting until it's too late.

And you can't let that happen, can you?

Think small

It's useful to think small when planning to collect your relative's memoirs. If you imagine a gigantic biography taking you from their cradle to now, you'll be overwhelmed. However, if you think of it as a simple gathering of memories, it appears as something much more manageable. It doesn't matter how many flowers there are in a bunch – and if you only manage to get a few, then that's still more than you would have had. Every memory is an achievement. There is no need to drive yourself insane with a massive goal. Think small. Think stories. Think snippets. Think slices of life. Your aim is to collect them.

If you then decide to publish them for your family, there are lots of ways in which you can do this. It's your choice. You can make a decision based on what you want to do with the memories. Every family is different, and every family has different aims and needs.

We'll look at all the different ways of getting the memories out there. If one of them appeals more than others, and you think it is too much of a technical challenge, remember that you don't have to do it yourself.

In the following chapters, you'll see how to go through the process step by step. We look at what to prepare, what to do, what to ask. There are guidelines and checklists to help you every step of the way. For those who want to polish the memories, we'll look at what makes a good story, and how to shape the memories into a satisfying structure. Finally, we'll explore how to do all the production side of things.

The Family Memory Kit builds on this book, with DVDs which explain the steps in detail, and demonstrations and examples of all the different possibilities.

The sections are:

1. Preparing
2. The Process
3. Putting it together
4. Publishing (sharing it with the family)

Chapter 2: What do I say when they make excuses?

The first thing that you should do is approach your relative and suggest that it's time for them to share their stories and wisdom with their family. Often, the first thing your relatives do is come up with a number of excuses as to why they shouldn't.

Some of these are easy to answer, and others may need careful arguments. Let's look at some of the statements that you may encounter:

- **Writing my memoir means my life is over**
- **It's too early**

What they're saying is that they don't feel old enough to start the process. Assure them that even though they have heaps of things still to learn and to experience, they have so much to share that it's never too early to start. Encourage them to start now, even though they may think they haven't lived enough yet. It may be encouraging if you say that you are also starting the process of capturing your own memories (and it would probably be a very good thing to do that in any case. What better gift to give to your children?)

- **I'm too boring (dull, normal)**
- **Who would want to hear about me?**
- **No one would care**

This one is easy. Today we are fascinated with memoirs. We search for our roots, we are insatiably curious about the past. We spread our emotions around on Facebook and other social media platforms, and we expect others to do the same. It's normal to reveal internal conflict, and it's fascinating to learn how others cope with theirs. Nobody is boring. Their life might seem normal to them, but it's genuinely unique. Everyone has had different experiences of growing up, different lives within a family, different hardships and triumphs. Some have travelled, some have experienced war, some have found their answers in spirituality. Everyone is different, and nobody is boring.

- **What's the point of returning to the past?**
- **I don't want to look back**
- **My life has been awful**
- **It's too sad to look back**
- **I have too many skeletons in my closet**
- **Let sleeping dogs lie**

- **It's too private**

What's the point of having a photo album? Surely, you can learn from your mistakes and successes! In every photo album are moments of pleasure, moments of pain, emotions that are complex and ambiguous.

Maybe it's fear of reawakening the painful parts that makes people hesitate. However, hard times don't disappear by pretending they never happened. Hard times teach us how to live in the present. It's because of the lessons of the past that we are who we are today.

Burying pain doesn't work. Pain works its way to the surface in all sorts of ways. Often, by remembering and working through the painful parts of the past, we can find some sort of resolution, some sort of acceptance and peace. Pain often loses its sting, and we are able to find the lessons that can be learned from it, the strengths that grew from it and that carried people through.

- **I refuse to criticise my parents**

It's sometimes hard for older people to be impartial when it comes to their own parents. They want to remember them a certain way, and often if they analyse the events and emotions of the past, this way of remembering is compromised. Sometimes we remember in black and white, but there are many, many shades of grey and lots of colours too! To re-form realistic memories of parents, we first have to accept that parents are real people with all the shades of emotion and the same range of good and bad decisions that we ourselves have made.

Daniel Siegel, a child psychologist, argues that we need our parents' stories to stay healthy ourselves, and this applies to everyone. We need the stories to be as authentic as possible. That way we can honour our parents for who they really are or were, rather than an idealised image or the opposite.

If you can get your relative to open up about their childhood – and they may need convincing – reassure them that you are not asking them to blame anyone for anything, but just show a clear picture of how they lived. What often happens, apart from being able to show that clear picture, is that your relative will develop a more compassionate and understanding relationship with their parents, long after they have passed away. In gathering these memories, you, yourself, will see your relative in a totally new light.

- **I can't remember all of that**
- **It's too overwhelming**

- **I can't write**
- **I can't get around to it**
- **I'm too busy**
- **It's too much work**

These are arguments about the time involved. Reassure your relative that you will not be taking up masses of time. Whatever time they can spare is fine. Even your regular weekly phone calls are a good time to tell stories – you can hold a recorder up to the phone if you like, or take notes. Whatever they can remember is valuable and precious.

- **People will think I'm full of myself**

That's an interesting argument. However, it's easy to explain that thinking and talking about yourself isn't a bad thing. So why is it okay to talk about yourself? You become more self aware, kinder, more compassionate. Without self-awareness we are stuck.

Also, when you tell your story to others, you're giving them a gift, and so, it would be selfish NOT to tell it!

- **It's too late**

They say that it's never too late. Sometimes, however, due to illness or circumstances, your relative may lose the ability to remember or to communicate. If you find yourself in a situation where you know you have limited time with your relative, encourage them to share whatever they can in the time that you have. If memories are fading, capture the ones that do rise to the surface. Even a small memento is better than nothing, and would be something to cherish.

One of the ways to counteract all those objections is to use them as springboards for conversation.

"Really? Tell me what you mean."

Try to get them to explain why remembering makes them feel uncomfortable.

Your job is to listen, to understand, to collaborate, to have a conversation. It's not an inquisition, but a loving sharing of memories – and after listening, be comforting and reassuring.

To counter the reasons that they are going to give you as to why they shouldn't do this, give them reasons why they should.

1. It can be therapeutic to remember and record the memories.

It's a wonderful way of healing, of getting in touch with your life, working through the bad times and finding the lessons, reliving the good times and reviving the joy.

2. It's for those who come after us, it's an important story to tell.

Help us all to understand your history, what you saw and experienced, and how it made you feel. We can understand so much from your life - your strength, your courage, your resilience, your knowledge and wisdom. It can be your gift to us.

3. Your children and grandchildren will feel close to you even when you're not here.

They will hear your voice and remember you. They will see the picture of your life as you have told it. As the years go by, and memories start to fade, they will have this to keep you close to them forever.

4. There are things that you may never get to tell your family at the time that they need to hear them.

If you do this, then you will always be there for them when they need it. Your children and grandchildren and great grandchildren will be able to learn from you, long after you are gone. They will be grateful that you have done this.

5. You'll be teaching your family not only about your own life, but about life in general.

Everything you went through has lessons in it for other people. You can help them to see how you coped and help them avoid making the same mistakes.

6. It can help make peace in the family.

Every family has its conflicts and rifts, but when people hear your side of the story, they will understand who you are and where you are coming from, and it may help them to understand and find peace. It's important to forgive and to ask for forgiveness, and to remember that a family is based on love, whatever else happens.

7. Sometimes we need to hear about the struggles of others in order to get over our own struggles.

My youngest son, Alex had some horrendous experiences with travel in America. However, he had with him the biography that my husband and sister-in-law wrote based on their mother's recordings. He read extracts from the biography, and instead of getting angry and lashing out, he realised that if his Baba could go through so much and survive, then what he was experiencing was nothing. It helped him see the humour and balance in an extremely stressful situation.

8. You are one of the bearers of tradition.

You have knowledge and skills to share, years of experience based on what has gone before, traditions that you uphold. You are one of the main sources of culture and history. You are important for the future.

Surely some of these reasons will convince your relative to share their memories with you.

Chapter 3: So what steps I should take?

The overall process is quite simple, and it shouldn't be overwhelming.

Basically, you're going to sit and talk with your relative, and record the conversation.

Don't get overwhelmed by the size of the task. You're going to record a few memories. Then a few more. Then a few more.

Eventually this will build up into a collection of memories in your relative's life. It would be impossible to collect a full record of their entire lives, so don't set yourself that impossible task.

It doesn't matter if the memories are out of order. You can put them in order later. It doesn't matter if they ramble all over the place. You can decide what to do about that at another time.

While you're with your relative, your job is to be present and to listen and to love.

Don't visualise the finished product, the end result. Just enjoy the process. One of the most important parts of this is the journey.

There are 4 main steps, and we will deal with each of them in subsequent chapters.

1. Preparing
2. Process
3. Putting it together
4. Publishing

1. Preparing

There are several things to do straight away (these are explained in the next chapter)

- Contact the person you want to help record their memoirs, and make a time to visit them. This will commit you to the process and it will mean that you've really made a start.

- Make copies of the pages that you will take with you. (These are all on the website in the resources section: www.TheFamilyMemorySite.com).

- Start your own research.

- Gather the tools you'll need (These are also in the resources section of the website.)
- Contact anyone else you want to help you.

2. The Process - recording the memories

Your first "memory" visit to your relative should introduce them to the project.

Encourage them, if they can, to fill in some of the sheets by themselves.

For the other regular visits, you take along your recording device (phone or digital recorder or computer). You chat about one or more of the triggers, or you ask one or more of the questions, and you record your relative's memories.

3. Putting it together - organising what you have

You don't need to wait until you have lots of memories to begin to organise them. You can do this as you go.

All you have to do is to make some sort of decision about how you want to put it all together (and you can change your mind or expand this later, if you want to.)

Depending on what you want to put together, go to that section of this book and follow the steps.

4. Publishing and sharing the memories

This is where you bring joy and connection to the rest of the family, or preserve the memories for your children and grandchildren to share.

Chapter 4: Preparation – let's get started!

Things to do first

The time to act is NOW

1. Contact the person and tell them that it's time to record their story.

Make that phone call or skype call. Write that letter or email. Make that first visit.

Let them know that you are going to help them to record their memories – and how important it is.

Do whatever it takes to convince them.

Keep the chapter open which deals with answering their objections. You may need it!

2. Prepare the tools you will need.

You can prepare your "tools" from the checklist on the website. www.TheFamilyMemorySite.com

Click on "Resources" and download "The Family Memory Toolkit." Tick what you have, and buy or borrow what you need.

3. Give your relative the list of things to put together, if they are able to do that on their own.

Use the checklist from the website and ask your relative to gather together things from the list.

You can gather whatever you have, too.

If necessary, you can help them to collect things.

4. Contact others who you would like to help you.

Maybe you would like your siblings or your children to help you on this.

Maybe you know people who have the documents and items you need.

Make a list of people, what they can help you with, and contact them.

5. You don't have to decide immediately how it will be published.

Don't put off collecting the memories because you don't know how you want to publish yet.

You can make that decision as you go.

The first step is to make an audio recording of your relative's voice as they tell their stories. The rest comes later.

6. Set a place and time for a visit.

Make the first appointment.

Put it in your diary.

Print out or photocopy:

From

www.TheFamilyMemorySite.com

On the "resources" page

- The list of things to collect (The Family Memory Toolkit)
- The Family Memory Decade Sheets
- The Family Memory Timeline
- The Family Memory Photo Log

Research

1. You don't have to do this before you start.

You can do this as you go (or not at all, if you don't want to.)

2. You don't have to do everything, only as much as you want to or have time for.

3. These are just suggestions to give you some ideas.

- Start by writing down what you know about your relative. Start with their birth date, wedding date, family's names, etc.

- Determine what gaps there are in your knowledge. What don't you know that you need to know?

- Google your relative.

- Learn more about the geographic area(s) where your relative lived.

- Read town and city histories to learn what life was like during your time period of interest.

- Research timelines of:
    - Wars
    - Natural disasters
    - Epidemics
- Investigate your relative's occupation(s) to get a better understanding of his/her daily activities.
- Read up on:
    - fashion
    - art
    - transportation
    - common foods
- Interview your living relatives about the person you are helping.
- Search your own closets for memorabilia.
- Ask other family members to search their cupboards.
- Ask your family members to share their photo albums (a good way to encourage them is to offer to scan the photos.)

- Interview your relative's close friends. Ask them what stands out about the person, what makes him or her unique and memorable. Don't shy away from asking tough questions or including material that doesn't show the person in the most favourable light. Everyone has faults.

- Visit your local library or conduct online research to find newspaper clippings, magazine articles and any additional information on your relative and pertinent facts and locations from his or her life. Birth records, obituaries, reviews of artistic works or performances and feature articles can help you to understand more and can also give you exact dates, names and locations, as well as a feel for your relative's era and environment.

- Research newspapers (now often digitised or on microfilm.)

- Research school year books (often available from the school.)

Read other memoirs!

You can learn a lot about memoir writing, and discover what you like (and don't like) from reading other people's memoirs.

Chapter 5: The process – let's record the memories!

This is the step that you have all been waiting for. You've done some preparation, and now it's time to start capturing your relative's memories. This is not supposed to be overwhelming. You record whatever they want to tell you based on a question or a trigger.

Go to:

www.TheFamilyMemorySite.com

Click on the "Club" Tab and join "The Family Memory Club" (It's free).

Click on "resources" and download The Family Memory Questions and Triggers.

What to do

The physical aspects of recording the memories are really very simple.

- Work out how the recording device works. You can use a digital recorder or your phone or your computer. See the latest suggestions on the resources page of the website.

- If you want to video the conversations, then play with the video to make sure you have everything ready.

- If you decide to use a video camera, put it on a tripod so the camera's in the background and not obvious all the time. Lots of people get a bit nervous talking with a camera there, but if it's not too invasive, they tend to forget it after a while.

- Take a camera to photograph any objects or documents that your relative may have, and maybe a few shots of your relative as he or she is talking to you.

1. **Before the first visit or at the first visit.**

(Of course this will not usually be "the first visit" to your relative! But this will be the first time for the memory project.)

- Give them copies of the Family Memory Decade Pages.
- Explain that these pages are for jotting down memories as they occur, not for completing in

chronological order. For example, if I think about the time I helped Grandpa with the gardening when I was 6, I would jot down 'gardening with Grandpa' on the 0-9 decade page. I would write 'my wedding day' on the 20-29 page, and so on. These will be really useful when you come to ask about your relative's memories.

- Give them the Family Memory Timeline.
- Help them, if necessary, fill in important dates on the timeline:
    - Birth
    - Marriage(s)
    - Birth of children
    - Graduation from school and college
    - Jobs
    - Deaths of parents and grandparents (and any other significant people)
    - Travel
    - Any other dates that are memorable in their life.

- (You can add other important historical events to the timeline, such as the Vietnam war, later.)

2. **On the recording days.**

   - Set up the recording device(s)
   - Test to check that it's working
   - Ask a question or use a trigger (you'll find these on the resources page of the website)
   - At the end of the day, AS SOON AS YOU GET HOME, back up your recordings. Save them onto the computer and make a back-up copy. It is MUCH better to be paranoid about losing the information than to lose it forever. (Thus speaks the voice of experience!)

Of course, if the distance is too far for a visit, then don't give up. It's still possible to gather memories by skype calls. These can be recorded, and you can ask much the same sort of questions. My mum, who is 84, skypes me all the time!

Failing that, there is always the phone, email and snail mail. If it's possible to use any means to capture those family memories, do it.

Some How-To Tips

- The conversations with your relative should be informal and enjoyable. Don't think of it as an interview. You'd like them to relax, open up and share their stories with you. Your main job is to listen and to encourage them. You should always be attentive and be ready to ask insightful and enthusiastic questions that show how interested you are. I always try to remain "fascinated" by all the topics. Most of the time, it isn't hard.

- Even though you're recording, it's important that you're both totally comfortable. It's okay to relax and laugh. That won't spoil the recording, it'll only add to the atmosphere. This is almost a "casual chat," and a cup of tea or coffee (or something stronger) is perfectly okay.

- Try to find a room to record in which is fairly quiet. Next door's lawn mower or the 'music' from the car across the road can be annoying when you play back the recording – and even a TV or a loud air conditioner can spoil an otherwise excellent recording.

- Make sure the seats are comfortable, with maybe a table where you can put photos or objects to look at.

- Everyone's situation will be different, but if it's possible, plan recording sessions once a week. More often may be tiring, and less often may mean that they forget what they've already talked about and go over old ground. That may happen in any case. However, you must make the best of the circumstances.

- Don't ever judge what they're saying or challenge them, and try not to direct the stories in a way that interests you. Remember that this isn't only for you, but for all the family.

- Make them feel they are special. They are!

- Be sensitive to the way the memories may make them feel. Some of the memories may make them sad or uncomfortable or angry, and you should be aware that this may happen. The story might be about a particularly painful time in their lives, or about someone they have since lost. If they get emotional, remember that you are not a therapist. It may be necessary to stop or redirect if this happens.

- Let them complete their thoughts. If they're silent for a while, that's okay. Maybe they will have difficulty phrasing exactly what they want to say and may have to say it in a few different ways. That's okay. You can always edit it or have it edited later.

- Ask them more about something if you're interested. It's okay to be curious and ask them to tell you more, or if you aren't sure who some of the people were in the story, ask.

Questions and triggers

There are many questions which you can ask, and many triggers which can spark memories.

The best questions are "open ended questions" which don't result in one-word or very short answers. For example, a question such as, "how old were you when you moved house?" is a closed question. It can be answered by "I was seven." A better question is, "What do you remember about moving house?' or "Tell me about when you moved house." Those are open-ended questions and are much more likely to elicit a story.

Good open-ended questions are:

"Tell me about…"

"What do you remember about…"

"What happened after that?"

"How did you feel about…"

"Can you explain that a bit more?"

"What was the reason…"

"What was the best thing about…"

"What was the worst thing about…"

"How did you used to…

Another good technique is to mirror their words. If they say "I used to like going to the Goose Fair." You could say, "The Goose Fair? That sounds interesting. What was the Goose Fair?" or "Tell me about the Goose Fair."

If they close off a topic with negatives, try to open up the discussion by using a positive. For example, if you ask about their school days, and they close the discussion by saying "I hated school," you could say, "Were there some days that you enjoyed?" or "Tell me about the friends you made there."

It's important to be as natural and relaxed as possible, and not to read the questions. It's a good idea to decide before you go which questions to ask today, but be flexible enough to let the memories take their own path. Remember, your questions are just triggers for memories.

What do you ask about?

For the sake of completeness, there's a huge list of questions in the resources section of the website. You can cover as many or as few as you want to – whatever is appropriate for your situation.

There's also a list of triggers, which can all be used as memory-joggers.

Photographs are, of course, excellent memory triggers, and you can ask lots of questions around a photo.

For example, the photo of the family in the garden in 1969 could spark a number of memories all by itself, but if it doesn't, I could ask my mother:

"What was it like to have Nana living with us?"

"Was it hard to have children so far apart in age?"

"How did you feel about the fashions back then?"

"Do you remember anything about when and where you bought your dress?"

"Tell me, what was the worst thing about my behaviour when I was 16?"

"How did Nana feel about leaving all her friends in England?"

I could ask about any of the five senses (touch, taste, smell, sight, hearing) or emotions.

"Do you remember what the garden smelled like?"

"What could you see in the garden? What were you looking at in the photo?"

"How did you feel on that day?"

"How do you feel looking back at that time in your life?"

I could ask about the other people in the family or the group.

"Where was Judith on that day?"

"Who was taking the photo?"

I could ask Mum to suggest dialogue.

"What were we talking about?"

There are so many possibilities just from a simple photo like this.

It's the small, almost insignificant details that add life to a memory. We want to see the dress Mum was wearing when she first saw Dad, and what her first impressions were of him. We want to know about how Dad smelled to her when he first held her in his arms. We want to know where she was when she realised she was pregnant for the first time. It's the tiny details that allow us to connect across the years, to find our points of similarity and difference.

A list of things to ask about

Not all of the questions from the website will be relevant to your circumstances.

It might be a good idea to go through them and delete the ones that have no relevance to you. That way you will be left with a list of questions which are appropriate.

You can add any more that you think of based on your own circumstances. Make a note of these, so you don't forget them. It's annoying to realise later that you didn't ask something you wanted to ask.

When you ask the questions, use words that you'd normally use, and ask them in a way that sounds natural to you.

There are many, many ways of eliciting memories. I don't claim to have an exhaustive list here. If you have some other wonderful ways that work, please contact me and let me know!

Chapter 6 Putting it together – let's organise the memories!

This chapter will introduce you to the many ways there are to record and publish your relative's memoirs.

The next few chapters will look at how to get the memories ready for publication, depending on which path you choose.

Of course, you don't have to make a decision straight away, but it'll help to keep the possibilities in mind while you're collecting the information.

For the first time in history, it's easy to record a person's memories with simple, inexpensive digital recording equipment.

It used to be that memoirs would have to be written, but this isn't the case any longer. You could write the memories down, but there are many other ways of preserving memories these days. Even if you want a written copy, you don't have to do it yourself. Once you've recorded the memories using audio equipment, the mp3 (audio) files can be transcribed – very affordably. You can then edit the transcription (or have it edited by someone else) and publish it.

You can make it into a digital story by adding film footage or photos.

You can publish it with photos in a photobook.

You can burn the files to a CD and include an audio recording with photos.

There are many, many possibilities.

Today you can even combine all of these and put them up on a website!

You can tell the story in your own words, or use the voice of your relative or those of other family members – or you can combine these.

You can copy documents and include them. You can have them translated, if necessary. You can add annotations and explanations. You can summarise or paraphrase them so others can understand them better.

You can stick to "just the bare facts," but don't feel that you have to be bound by the bare essentials. If you want to, you can add creative elements such as descriptive scenes or imagined dialogue.

The way you put the project together is absolutely up to you.

Remember, anything you can't do yourself, you can get someone else to do for you. The services are available cheaply, or you can pay more for dedicated professional help.

What do you want to do with the Family Memories?

How you put it all together will depend on what you see as the end purpose of the family memories.

It may be, if all you want to do is share some memories with close family members, that a simple photocopied booklet is all you really want to put together.

You may want to make a hardback book to last for generations.

You may want to put up a website or make a video.

You should take into account your own time constraints and obligations, the end purpose, your interests and your schedule. You also have to take into account what materials you have to work with, and what you would like to include.

It's important to decide on something that is doable. You don't want to overstretch your ambitions, and have a half-finished project forever.

So let's look at some of the possibilities.

In later chapters we will explore exactly how to go about these.

Audio memories

If you want to keep the files as audio without transcribing them, you still have several possibilities:

- Audio files on a website
- CDs
- MP3 files for iPods
- Family podcast

Suggestions to help you with these are on the resources page of the website.

www.TheFamilyMemorySite.com

Written memories

There are lots of possibilities if you want to write the memories.

- Traditional book
- Ebook
- PDF files
- Blog or website
- A journal
- A family newsletter
- Letters to individual family members
- A heritage album
- Scrapbooks
- A loose leaf binder
- Photobooks
- A cookery book with memories included
- A family magazine

Video memories

If you want to put the story onto video, there are quite a few options:

- Digital stories with photos and film footage, with you narrating, or with your relative narrating.
- Video of your relative telling the story, with photos interspersed.

- Voice over of film footage. Your relative can do the voice-over, or you can do it yourself.
- Video can be placed on a website.
- You can make a CD ROM or DVD compilation of files.

Other ideas

There are other possibilities, limited only by your imagination.

- A website can include all the various forms of memory recording.
- You may want to make a family exhibition, where at a special event such as a birthday or Christmas or a family reunion, all the memories are available for people to share.
- Time capsule – a physical storage container (as simple as a shoebox or a much fancier version) which contains copies of the memories and other significant objects.
- A secret facebook site can allow all the family to comment of the memories that you upload.

The title

If you are going to publish the collection of memories, then you may want to give it a title. It may be something as simple as "Jane Smith's memories" or you may want to pick something more evocative.

Whatever you choose is fine. If you eventually send it to a publisher, they will probably change the title anyway.

A few notes before we start

1. Think Small

A collection of memories is not a biography. It's a collection of memories. If you want to go on to write a biography of your relative, there's nothing to stop you - but this project is much smaller than that. It simply aims to collect memories so that snippets of and insights into your relative's life are preserved for your family.

2. A note about truth

It is important to be as truthful as possible.

The emotional truth of a situation is what makes it reach and connect across the years. If a story deals with emotions – love, loneliness, anger, confidence, vulnerability, rejection and acceptance – it will make a connection not only with us, but with generations to come.

Facts are important, but the emotional truths are in many ways more important. They are the heart of the story.

It's probable that not everything that you're told will be 'the truth, the whole truth and nothing but the truth.' It's the nature of the human mind that we forget things. We remember things that didn't actually happen, and we report stories that were told to us which may or may not be the strict truth. In some cases, we tell lies.

The more documents you can find in your research, the more you can check facts, if you want to. Sometimes, however, the story – the memory – is to be preferred to the reality. You may not be praised for your efforts at uncovering the "truth."

We are dealing in memories. This is the way your relative remembers it. This is what makes them who they are.

You may speak to other relatives who claim "That isn't the way it happened!" and that's okay, too. If people remember things in different ways, that's normal. Be okay with that.

Sometimes the very controversy of a situation within a family IS the story. It can be what makes an event memorable. At Christmas, in 1995, my eldest son, Taras, broke all the carob Christmas tree decorations. My youngest, Alex, was blamed for it because Taras wouldn't own up. That's what I think happened. Each of my three children has a differing account of that event, however. Which one is "true"?

To give another example – none of my children agrees on whose fault it was that Alex split his head open on a chest of drawers in 1989. However, talking about it over the years has brought the story out of the painful and into the humorous, because they refuse to agree. Alex has forgiven the others because it's a shared joke now. This is what makes families closer.

Memories are not a definitive version of truth. They are what they are. They are what the person remembers.

Grouping the stories

If you've collected many memories, you may want to group them. Here are some possibilities for grouping them. One or more may appeal to you.

1. Chronological order

You could use a simple chronological order. Start with the early memories and just go through your relative's life, following the decade sheets or the timeline.

This is a nice, simple solution and could work really well.

The only problem is that you may find that there are some stories that span many years and it's difficult to decide where to put them.

2. Themes

For the purpose of this book, I'm using the word "theme" to mean an idea that can bind several stories together.

There may be stories of "different sorts of love" or "times of hardship," "Stories of forgiveness" or "silly things children have done" which can all be gathered together in a group.

Again, you will find that there are some odd stories that don't fit into any particular group, and these can be grouped in some other way – chronologically, for example.

3. Types of Stories

Another way of grouping stories is by topic.

You may have a group of stories about different people, or places that were special. Here is a list to start thinking about:

Character stories:

Stories about relationships with a single person. These may look at that person's influence in your relative's life, or might honour them if they have died.

Adventure stories:

Exciting events in your relative's life. Challenges overcome and lessons learned.

Accomplishment stories:

Achieving a goal, desire / struggle / achievement, overcoming obstacles.

Stories about Place:

Places that have meant something to, or affected, your relative in some way. Where is home? Where were you when…? These stories connect your relative to places that can be visited and shared in future years by their descendants.

Work stories:

Stories about their jobs and what they did in their day-to-day lives. How did they do things differently? What insights did they learn?

Recovery stories:

Sharing the challenges that they have overcome. Health crises. Personal obstacles. Insights learned along the way.

Love stories:

Romance, partnership, family. What was it like to hold your baby in your arms? How close did you feel to your siblings? The first time you fell in love.

Discovery stories:

Things they learned in their life that they want to share. How they discovered certain truths in their lives.

4. The shape of a story

Remember at school you were taught that a good story has a beginning, a middle and an end? It's true for memories, too.

If you're going to do more than just copy the audio recordings for everyone to listen to – if you are going to put them together in some way – you may need to think a bit about the shape, the structure of the story.

You may not think that, in your circumstances, this is important – and that's okay. You may not want to change the memories in any way. What Mum said, word for word, is what you want.

Some readers will want to write the memories down, or make digital stories, or put them together into a photobook. If you intend to publish the memories in any way, you might like to think about structure.

There are a few different patterns which suit different sorts of stories. These patterns are found in written stories, photo stories and video stories, and you can follow the patterns if you think they would be useful.

I have summarised a few of them on the website.

www.TheFamilyMemorySite.com

Click on "Resources" and download 'The Family Memory Stories'

Should you worry about legal issues?

At this stage, don't worry too much about writing about other people and using their names. Don't worry about offending them or getting things wrong. Just worry about getting it down. YOU CAN CHANGE EVERYTHING LATER IF YOU HAVE TO. You can change names, dates, times, places and details later. You can run it by a lawyer, literary agent or publisher later.

You may need to concern yourself with legal issues one day, if you are going to publish the memories to the world. However, if it is just for your family, you may never have to worry about this.

Include an index

If your relative tells lots of stories, it's good to make an index as you go along. That will make everything so much easier to find later.

An index should include the names of the people in the stories, the places the stories happened, and the type of event that the memory is about. If you write these three things down for each memory as you record it, it will be easy to compile an index later. There's an index template in the resources section on the website.

Chapter 7 Publishing Audio Memories

You've recorded your audio, and now you want people to listen to it.

Today there's simple audio editing software that you can get for your computer that will help you here.

Editing

Editing can help you to:

- Rearrange the audio into the order that you want
- Break it up into smaller pieces or chapters
- Add music tracks
- Add sound effects
- Remove stammers and stutters (Only if you want to. No judgment. If Nana is okay with her stutter, you can leave it in. The grandkids may be interested to know that Nana had a stutter, just like they do!)
- Remove long pauses

- Add voice-overs from different people
- Adjust the volume

The editing software

- Some computer manufacturers supply audio software as part of purchasing a computer.
- Audio editing software is normally included with digital audio recorders as part of the purchase and can be installed on your computer.
- There are several free programs available.
- You can buy software, too.

There is a guide to audio software in the resources section of the website.

Music

Music stirs up an emotional response, so it's probably something that you have considered adding to your audio.

Here are a few pieces of advice about using music:

1. Don't use copyrighted music if your audio track will ever be published – unless, of course, you pay for it.

Simply, if you'll ever make any money out of the recording, you should have permission to use the music. Fortunately, numerous companies have developed copyright-free music collections. Some of these are listed in the resources section of the website.

However, if only your family is ever going to listen to it, don't worry too much. If you're really worried, you could also print a disclaimer on the CD cover, or record yourself saying one onto the tape. An example is in the resource section of the website.

2. If you use music with lyrics to add to your story, that's fine, but don't try to put them under your voice recording because the two will work against one another. Most people can't listen to the lyrics of a song and listen to a voice recording at the same time. There may also be a conflict of meaning between what your relative is saying and the words of the song.

3. Instrumental music is a safer choice and is usually very effective. You could even ask your relative if they have favourite pieces of classical or instrumental music they think might go with their story.

Outsourcing

If you feel that anything is too difficult, you can always send it to a professional audio editor. Suggestions are in the resources section of the website.

Publishing

This is why we have made the collection of memories, so it is important to know what to do with the audio files in order to share them.

- Physical – Transfer the audio to a CD, DVD, USB drive or MP3 player. This is good if absolute privacy is a must.

- Digital – Share audio via email or on audio sharing sites. The good thing about audio sharing sites is that the files can be accessed by everyone and downloaded. You can put the files up on your website, or use a sharing tool. These are discussed in the resources section of the website.

- Podcast – There are links to instructions for this in the resources section of the website.

Keeping the data safe

Keep your own copies of the recordings, and be sure to keep a backup copy.

Some people like to store their data and link to it from a website (examples are in the resources section of the website.)

Once the audio files are edited and published, they can be sent to be transcribed, or used as resources to create or complement any of the written or video options discussed in the next chapters.

Chapter 8 Publishing Written Memories

Because your project is so individual, you can put it together however you want. You may, therefore, decide to have some parts of it which are written. You may want to include different styles such as narratives, essays, poems, scenes, letters or speeches, especially if your relative wrote some of these. There are lots of possibilities if you want to write the memories.

Traditional book

Either self-published or using a publisher (see the exciting bonus in the resources section of the website.)

Ebook

These can be uploaded to an ebook publishing site and published yourself (see the exciting bonus in the resources section of the website.)

PDF files

These are files that you can share with other members of the family. They can be emailed or uploaded to a website, and because they are in .pdf format, they will always look the same on any computer.

Blogs on a website

A blog can be installed on a family memories website. You can make a website yourself with simple website builders (some easy ones are mentioned in the resources section of the website.) You can, of course get someone to do it for you – either a knowledgeable relative or a web designer.

You can publish the memories on the blog, as you collect them.

A journal

You can publish a journal every month or every quarter and include all the memories that you have collected.

A family newsletter

An email or physical newsletter is a great idea to keep the family in touch with what you are doing.

Letters to individual family members

If certain memories are in the form of messages to individual family members, it would be a great idea to send them as a personal letter. You could use email, but a snail-mail letter would be a good idea, too (although beware of sending original documents in the post!)

A heritage album

In this, you can include the written copies of the memories, but also copies of documents, photos, maps – anything, in fact. It can be as full a collection as you feel like putting together.

Scrapbooks

These are much like a heritage album, but each page is carefully decorated and is often a work of art in its own right.

A loose-leaf binder

Often the collection can be stored in a loose-leaf binder, which allows you to include plastic sleeve inserts of CDs, photos, copies of memorabilia, etc. They can be re-sorted, or extra things inserted, whenever you like.

Photobooks

A photobook can be made online or the software downloaded to your computer (see the resources section of the website.) Photos and stories can be included and the book published for a reasonable cost. These can be very high quality for a relatively low price, and archival paper is an option. However they're very labour-intensive.

A cookery book with memories and photos included

This type of book makes a great heirloom for all members of the family. Grandma's recipes may be used by generations to come.

A magazine

This is a collection of memories and memorabilia published in magazine format.

When you write, you should consider if you want to write it as yourself, reporting and commenting on your relative's life, or whether you want to write it from their point of view, as if you were them.

Will you write each memory in the present tense, as if it is happening now? Or will you write about it in the past tense?

There is no one perfect universal answer. You must choose the one that feels right for you.

You don't have to write (someone else can do it.)

Once you have the recorded memories, you don't have to transcribe them yourself. (See the resources section on the website for suggestions.)

If you can train one of the dictation programs to recognise your relative's voice, the computer software can do it for you.

If you have the audio files, you can send them to various online providers and someone will transcribe them for you. This can be very affordable.

You can give everything to a ghostwriter, and they can do it all for you.

After the writing is done.

You should consider having someone edit the writing.

There are 3 main levels of editing,

1. Self editing
2. Development editing (where the editor gives you ideas about content, structure, direction etc.)
3. Line editing (where the editor corrects your grammar, sentence structure, spelling etc.)
4. Proofreading

There is no point in doing these out of order.

Download the Family Memory Editing Tips from the resources section of the website:

www.TheFamilyMemorySite.com

The first pass through should always be done by you. Get the manuscript into the best order that you can. You can ask yourself the questions from the Family Memory Editing Tips.

Now is the time to review and correct the appearance (formatting) of your work.

- Consider line spacing,
- Look at the font and size that you have used for the headings of chapters and sections of work.

Now is also the time to decide where to insert photographs, letters, copies of letters, and so on.

The second pass can be done by a family member. Give them the same list of questions (from the website), and ask them to be honest.

You can, of course find a professional editor who will do this for you.

The third pass should be done by someone who can give you a really good line edit. This should not be you, if at all possible. Often we are too close to the work to see the details. The best line edits are done by people with good attention to detail, who have never read the work before.

The final pass before publication is the proofreading. This is a check to make sure that nothing has been missed.

Publishing: a special BONUS surprise!

If you're interested in publishing your collection of memoirs, I have a special surprise for you. I have put together a video which you can access FREE from the download section of the website! It is part of my *Write your Book with Dr Rie* series, and it looks at all the ways of publishing a book. There is also a workbook, a tips and tricks video, and tips and tricks worksheets.

Other places for publication:

You can send the memories away to nostalgia and senior-oriented magazines and blogs.

Some journals focus on pets, or disabilities, or veterans or hobbies or other interests, and stories from the "old days" are often very welcome.

Legal issues

If there are stories about other people who are still alive, be careful before you choose to publish the stories. There may be legal consequences.

Either get a "release" from the people concerned, or change the names or leave them out.

You don't want to spoil a relationship or have to deal with a lawsuit just because you want to publish your relative's stories. A sample release form is available in the resources section of the website.

Chapter 9 Publishing Video Memories

If you want to put the story onto video, there are quite a few options:

Digital stories with photos and film footage, with you narrating, or with your relative narrating.

Digital stories are made in a few easy steps.

1. Choose the story. It should take about 3 −5 minutes to tell.

2. Write the story (or make a few notes, so you don't lose track of the story)

3. An alternative way to go about making a digital story is to make a visual narrative. You line up photos on the table, and decide what story you want to tell about those photos. You then write the story. There are advantages and disadvantages to this method. The advantage is that the story almost tells itself. The disadvantage is that you could be left with holes in your story that you may have to find other images to fill.

4. Record the story on audio. Either you or your relative could be the narrator. (For the sake of posterity, it's probably best for your relative to do this if at all possible.)

5. Transfer the audio files to the computer.

6. Import it as an audio track on a movie editing program (suggestions and links to instructions are in the resources section of the website.)

7. Add photos or pictures.

8. Put in transitions and effects if you feel like it.

9. Add a music track (without lyrics) if you want to.

10. Export it to a common video format, so that your intended audience can open it on their computer. Burn it to DVD or put it on a USB stick, or upload it to a website.

Video of your relative telling the story with photos interspersed

1. Record your relative with a video camera as he or she tells the story.

2. Import the footage into a movie editing program (suggestions and links to instructions are in the resources section of the website.)

3. Extract the audio onto its own audio line.

4. Add photos to the project.

5. Put in transitions and effects if you feel like it.

6. Add a music track if you wish - without lyrics.

7. Export it to a common video format.

8. Burn to DVD or put it on a USB stick, or upload it to a website.

Voice-over of film footage.

Your relative can do the voice-over, or you can do it yourself.

This is a wonderful project, if your relative has a lot of film or video of their lives or their children's lives.

One of the most beautiful and memorable times in my life was sitting with my parents when they were 84 and 86, as they shared their memories while watching the film footage they had shot of their children growing up. What a treasure for me and my siblings, and all our children and grandchildren!

1. Transfer the footage into digital files for the computer. You may need to outsource it, but it is possible to do it yourself (suggestions in the resources section of the

website.) If you have it done professionally, the quality may be better, though.

2. Edit the video footage and film into order, and cut out any badly damaged parts. You can use any movie editing program.

3. For the next bit, you will need a program to record what is on your desktop. Suggestions are in the resources section of the website. Play the edited footage, and record your relative's reaction to the footage, or ask them to do a voice-over for you.

4. Export the files.

5. Transfer it to DVD or USB or upload it to a website.

Chapter 10: Other Ideas for Publishing

There are other possibilities, limited only by your imagination.

A website

A website can include all the various forms of memory recording.

You can create your own website, using any website builder (see the resources section of the website.)

On your website, you can include any of the audio recordings or video recordings you have made.

You can upload your text files for others in the family to read.

You can upload photos, documents, letters, in fact anything that is of significance to your family.

The documents and photos can be scanned and placed in a gallery or slide show on the site.

Movies and videos can be edited and placed online with video hosting services (see the resources section of the website), where they can then be accessed via the site.

Imagine how this would enrich the stories that your relative has told!

What a resource that would be!

A CD ROM or DVD compilation of files

If you don't want to put everything on a website, you can make a compilation of all the files on a DVD or CD ROM or USB stick. Then you can present them in this format to any family member.

A family exhibition

At a special event such as a birthday or Christmas or a family reunion, all the memories are available for people to share.

You can put up photos, play music and videos, bring in the memorabilia, have maps, and all the rest of your research – and everyone can bring in what they have to contribute. This is a project that the whole family can participate in.

Imagine your next Christmas, with everyone sharing their own memories of "the day we got the puppy" or "that Christmas right after the baby was born". Everyone would have different memories of just one event, and they could all laugh and reminisce, and the grandchildren could learn about their parents' and grandparents' lives before they were born. This is a wonderful family bonding activity.

A time capsule

A time capsule is a physical storage container (as simple as a shoebox or a much fancier version) which contains copies of the memories and other significant objects.

Once again, it is something that the whole family could contribute to.

A time capsule can be created for any special event, and all the family could bring something to place in it which relates to either the event, or – if it's a birthday or a wedding anniversary – to the person or people that are celebrating the event.

Once again, the family bonding that's possible far outweighs the possible organisational issues.

A family secret facebook page

It's possible to open a secret facebook page. Only family members or people you invite will be able to see what is on that page. The instructions for setting up such a page are in the resources section of the website. On that page you can post videos and audio files and pictures and stories to share with the family.

Conclusion: So what do I do right now?

So you see, the whole process is really very simple.

1. Getting ready
2. Getting it done
3. Getting it together
4. Getting it out there

There are only the four main parts, and if anything's too difficult, you can often get help or outsource it.

To recap what the four parts involve:

1. Preparing

There are several things to do straight away -

• Contact your relative and make a time to visit them.

• Make copies of the pages that you will take with you

• Start your own research (optional)

• Gather the tools you will need

• Contact anyone else you want to help you.

3. The Process - Recording the memories
- Your first "memory" visit to your relative should introduce them to the project.
- Encourage them, if they can, to fill in some of the sheets by themselves.
- For the other regular visits, you take along your recording device.
- Chat about one or more of the triggers, or you ask one or more of the questions.
- Record your relative's memories.

3. Putting it together - Organising what you have

You don't need to wait until you have lots of memories to begin to organise them. You can do this as you go.

All you have to do is to make some sort of decision about what you want to put together (and you can change your mind or expand this later, if you want to.)

Depending on what you want to put together, go to that section of this book and follow the steps.

4. Publishing and sharing the memories

This is where you bring joy and connection to the rest of the family, or preserve the memories for your children and grandchildren to share.

So the FIRST STEP is to contact your relative and make a time to visit them. You can do that NOW.

This is not the time for waiting until another day. Think about it. None of us know how much time we have, and how much time we have with our loved ones. It is never too early to start on this project – and, while our relatives are alive, it is never too late.

In one of my favourite books and films, *The Lord of the Rings: The Fellowship of the Ring*, JRR Tolkien's character, Gandalf, says something very profound which I use as one of my life-messages,

> "All we have to decide is what to do with the time that is given to us."

I have a friend who was getting very frustrated by her visits to her mother. Her mum had Alzheimer's and often didn't remember her. I suggested that she record her mum, if she was in a speaking mood, and see what she could remember. She took her mum's family photo album and recorded her mum as she remembered the past. Remembering the past was a soothing and affirming activity. Many people with dementia may not remember what happened 45 minutes ago, but they can clearly recall their lives 45 years earlier. My friend lost her mum shortly afterwards, but the stories she was able to capture are very precious to her.

My parents have started writing their memoirs by themselves. If they finish, well and good, but if they don't, they have preserved some memories for the family. I also have a wonderful DVD of their home movies with their own voice-over recorded when they were 84 and 86. I am collecting memories and stories from them whenever I can.

I didn't manage to do this for my grandmother. Nana's memories died with her. There are many questions I wish I had asked, and many stories I wish I had captured, but it is too late.

It is NOT too late for you!

You know you SHOULD do this

You WANT to do this

You CAN do this

So do it!

Don't let it be too late for you and your family.

It's your heritage.

It's your legacy,

and NOW is the time to start.

Give them the present of the past… for the future.

References and Resources

A very useful list of reference material and resources is in the resources section of the website.

www.TheFamilyMemorySite.com

To download any of the resources, go to the website, join "The Family Memory Club" (it's free) and click on the resources you would like.

If you would like a hard copy of the resources, please contact:

info@thefamilymemorysite.com

Testimonials

The Family Memory Project is a simple step-by-step process to record your family's history for future generations. Rie Natalenko has written a precise step-by-step guide in an easy-to-follow format to help me to be part of a small project to preserve the emotions, sights and relevant stories of my family that we will cherish forever. The guides and question prompts have been invaluable to help me – and my family – to get started. This will be an incredible journey for all of us!

Susan Reid

I've been thinking of recording my parents' memories for some time but didn't know where to start or what to cover. The list of questions and the decade pages to encourage my parents to think and prepare for our sessions made it exciting instead of overwhelming. Dr Rie made the project accessible instead of daunting and I'm proud to be undertaking this project on behalf of my siblings and for future generations.

Susan Wallis

The Family Memory Project is a gateway into my family's history. Since having children, I've longed to know and understand my parents and their ancestors. Having the structure and guidance to interview my mother has enabled me to piece together her history, which previously felt like a garbage bag of post-it notes. Understanding where she has come from and her perspective on her world has helped me cultivate compassion for my mother, which has shifted our relationship. I'm thankful to have the opportunity to record her memories for my children, nieces and nephews, so that they may better understand who they are and their place in the world.

    Gretel Van-Lane

The project was inspirational and made me take action. I had thought of recording Rose's stories but had never got around to it. The Family Memory Project gave me a structure that was easy to implement and I have now made a start. Rose loves telling stories of her past so I am sure this is going to be an enjoyable process for both of us, and a fantastic legacy for the great grandchildren.

    Catherine Saunders

As a person with a number of family photos of people I know nothing about, The Family Memory Project has been a wonderful catalyst. Everything is there to get you started and keep you focused on getting those stories captured so that other family members can enjoy and share the stories behind the photos. It provides a very useful structure and I particularly loved the trigger questions. It helped me to have more in-depth conversations with my Mum than I would have had otherwise, and has given her some impetus to have the conversations that would otherwise be left until 'one day.' I know my own children will enjoy finding out about their heritage and it will make their relatives that much more real to them.

Sharron Spratt

I've been meaning to record our history for ages but as my eyesight failed it became harder to tackle, and I just didn't know where to start.

Sharing the memories with my family has been an easy process and I'm glad there's a record to fill in the gaps our family tree records don't cover.

Phil A (Age 80)

The Family Memory Book and Kit are unique and precious and should be compulsory for all families! Rie has a wonderful, personable way of stepping you through every aspect so it makes the project easy and fun. I am so glad that I have now begun to record parts of my mum's life, which we will now have forever!

Don't just think about doing this 'one day' - start today and let Rie help you!

Judeth Wilson

Thank you so much for writing this book. I have been trying to trace my family history and it has been frustrating as most records are Eurocentric. I think this will be much more valuable and important for my family especially as so many of my older family members are beginning to fail.

Margaret Chung

Congratulations on a fabulous and well needed project for people :) this is wonderful. My dear 93-year-old nan passed away 3 weeks ago and all we have are verbal memories and stories.

This work you're doing is fantastic!

Emma Franklin Bell

I found the book easy to read and follow, all the steps were set out logically and in an easy to read format. If the steps are followed the project becomes a delightful exercise in recording memories, experiences and events.

Several years ago, for his birthday, I gave my father a very special pen and a beautifully bound notebook for him to write down his memories and recollections of his life. Dad promised me he would and I took him at his work. I would sometimes ask Dad how he was getting on and got a very noncommittal answer. Sadly Dad passed away last year, and when we were packing up his things with Mum the pen and notebook were in his drawer untouched.

This illustrates to me the importance of having a set of steps to follow and an end goal. It has also given me the 'push' needed to start recording Mum's memories before it is too late.

I am a Funeral Celebrant, often called upon a to meet with a family at a very difficult time in their life. Often a family will tell me they do not have a family member who can do a eulogy for their loved one and it is left to me to try to find out information on the life of the deceased (sometimes it is like pulling teeth) so that their life can be celebrated in a fitting and suitable manner. Sometimes it is not until after the ceremony has been held that the family will tell me something they have discovered that would have made such a difference to the ceremony.

I feel that if more and more families followed the Family Memory Project method it would make life far easier for them in their time of need.

Jacqueline Slater

www.ingramcontent.com/pod-product-compliance
Ingram Content Group UK Ltd.
Pitfield, Milton Keynes, MK11 3LW, UK
UKHW022215230426
12048UKWH00016BA/860